ISBN9789994569274

Published by Brookridge Publishing PO Box 9053, Walvis Bay Namibia Tel.: +264-64-221816
brookridgepublishing@gmail.com

Tying to Make Sense of It, Memoirs of a New Generation Zimbabwean

By T.F.Tagarira

INTRODUCTION

Prior to writing this book I have been warned not to do so for my own personal safety,but what is the point of writing a book if noone is going to read it. In this book I am shedding light to the plight of my generation and seeking genuine engagement in the political process. In this book I am telling my life's story and how the Zimbabwean crisis shaped my outlook and perspective on life. I am part of an angry generation. A generation that feels alienated from the political process. We have been through many trials and tribulations which are not of our making and we are bitter. These trials and tribulations have shaped our political perception and maturity. For most of us it seems that our politicians have been seduced by the adulterous prostitute of materialism. They are fattening their own pockets at the expense of the young generation. They feel threatened by my generation but we are not their enemy,we are children of the motherland too. In the past years the nation descended into chaos. Many young Zimbabweans were scattered beyond the borders only to find themselves foraging in foreign lands for a penny and sometimes a dollar,all for the upkeep of people back home. Today,young Zimbabweans are suffering in their own land,but why should we suffer? Why cant the doors of opportunities be accessible by all of Zimbabwe's children. We should all have an equal chance. Success should not be reserved for the who's who only. Success should not be reserved for the honorable comrades,their families and associates only. A poor child in the ghetto or rural village should have an equal opportunity as the rich child of any affluent politician. The very politicians should not forget that they too came from the ghetto's and villages. They too started off with nothing. They have a moral obligation not to block the way to success of the youth. Everyone should have an equal chance to pursue their hopes and dreams. People should not fail because the politicians failed them. The politicians have a moral responsibility to create a fair environment in which anyone can pursue their dreams despite political affiliation, age or gender. We are all Zimbabweans. Why should any Zimbabwean be more superior than the other?

Regards.

The New Generation.

This book is dedicated to the country I love,Zimbabwe.

CHAPTER 1

BACKGROUND.

"I am telling my story because I can no longer stomach the silence."

(* figure of speech) My life has been a battle to reclaim hope for a better tomorrow. I was pushed to the brink of hopelessness during the Zimbabwean crisis. My reality became agonizing and the prospect of a better tomorrow is what kept me going. In Zimbabwe I am a *Plebeian because I committed a crime; I was born after the war and for that I am considered politically immature to express my opinion.

I was born under the *Patrician rule and there are many others like me. We are a bitter and traumatized generation. All we want is an equal chance to pursue happiness in the land of our fore fathers. This book is my story,a mere tip of a much bigger Iceberg. There are many untold stories of the*Plebeian struggle and I am telling my story because I can no longer stomach the silence.

I wrote this book at breaking point. When Zimbabwe descended into crisis I found myself foraging in foreign lands for my brothers keep,but deep down in my soul I longed for my country. I found myself wondering in the darkness,searching for light but there was only darkness,only sadness. I didn't burn Zimbabwe but I paid a price for its destruction. Those who burned it,the*Patricians,were busy looting the empires treasure vaults amidst the chaos.

The scars of Zimbabwe's destruction will forever be engraved in my heart. I discovered that the only certain thing in life is uncertainty and death. However,It wasn't always like that. For a short while,life was sweet but the honeymoon ended when the *Patricians crushed the mighty titanic.

Suddenly,what was meant to be a nice voyage became a nightmare.

Many of the *Patricians filled up all the life boats with their children and stolen treasures and they sailed away to financial paradise. As for us, the *Plebeians,well,we had to scrounge for survival. I jumped onto an ice cap to avoid sinking into the fiery waters of oblivion. For a while I drifted on the ice cap but then it started melting away due to political global warming. My life became a survival series of jumping from one melting ice cap to another.

I am tired of jumping and drifting. I am hoping for a miracle that somehow I will drift onto a beautiful paradise island of peace and opportunity. In the meantime,I will tell you my life story. I shall begin by telling you my family history because it's a part of me that I can't exclude from this memoir. In the beginning,before I was born my ancestors lived and prospered in the land. That was before the white man came along with their union jack flag. Long before ZanuPF or MDC were formed. My father told me this history of my ancestors. Its a story that has been passed on from one generation to another.

I am from the Shumba,Gurundoro tribe. In the old days my great great great great grandfather was a king of the Gurundoro people. His kingdom was in the land that is now Harare,the capital city of Zimbabwe. He lived in harmony with other clans and he ruled his people justly and fairly. Our people were skilled farmers,hunters and cattle herders. They thrived in their land and lacked for nothing. One fateful day Vasinamabvi,"the white man" came with their union jack flag and renamed the land Salisbury. Mambo Gurundoro Tagarira saw that he was no match for the white people's guns. He decided to save his people.

He moved them to Chivhu and they settled in the area now called Marondamashanu on top of a mountain,a good defense strategy in those days. After a while a white farmer came and settled on a vast piece of land adjacent to the mountain. One day , the white man came to see Mambo Gurundoro and asked him for protection of his wife and child.

He was traveling to Suid Africa and in those days going to South Africa took months. The white man left for Suid Africa and left his wife and child under the care of Mambo Gurundoro. Months went by and after a year the white man had not returned from Suid Africa. Mambo Gurundoro consulted his dare "leadership council" to decide what to do with the white man's wife and daughter as they feared that he had been devoured by lions or killed on his way to Suid Africa.

They decided invite the wife and daughter of the white man to come and live amongst the Gurundoro people on top of the mountain for better protection. The white woman and her daughter agreed and they adjusted well to the Gurundoro way of life. One day,after many years the white man came back and was infuriated when he discovered that his wife had become a Gurundoro. He went to Salisbury and fetched a massive army of white man.

A Svikiro "oracle" of the Gurundoro people told King Gurundoro to vacate the mountain as he foresaw death. Mambo Gurundoro was fed up with always moving his people at the white mans whim. He decided to stay and fight. He knew the mountain provided good defense and they planned to hurl down rocks at the white army if they tried to climb to the mountaintop. On the fateful day,Mambo Gurundoro's first son left before sunrise on a hunting expedition. That morning the Gurundoro people woke up to mayhem.

The white men had climbed to the mountaintop during the night and started shooting every man in sight including male children. Mambo Gurundoro and all the males who were on the mountaintop died that fateful day at the hands of the white man. Later in the day Mambo Gurundoro's first son came back from his hunting expedition only to find piles of dead bodies of all the males of his tribe. Only the women had been spared and most of them fled the mountain top. Mambo Gurundoro's first son named the mountain Makumimavi,meaning that countless people died on that mountain.

In his later years, Mambo Gurundoro's son was taught how to peg farms by the white man,a task which he performed diligently. One day when they finished pegging the last farm in the area the white people asked him to choose a small scale farm of his liking as he had done them a great service. He chose the farm next to the Makunimavi mountain and to this day this is still the Tagarira family farm in Marondamashanu,Chivhu. The mountain is still called Makumimavi. Sometimes,I wonder what life would have been like for the Gurundoro people had the white man not interfered,but that's not the story I want to tell you. I want to tell you about my trials and

tribulations as a new generation Zimbabwean.

CHAPTER 2:

THE EARLY DAYS

"Many of us walk around with smiles on our faces but deep down we are sick and tired of bearing the scars of a crisis that was not of our making."

Many young people of my generation feel disenfranchised from the political process. Many of us walk around with smiles on our faces but deep down we are sick and tired of bearing the scars of a crisis that was not of our making. In this book I tell my own story and how it has shaped my political maturity and perception. I was born on the 27th of October in 1983 at Madamombe clinic in Mahusekwa district in Marondera,a small town about 90 km outside Harare. I was born at 4:00 am on a beautiful Thursday morning.

Like any newborn baby I cried when I came out of my mothers womb. My parents were extremely proud that happy day. They had created a new life and I was their first bundle of joy,their first miracle,their first son. They named me Tendai Frank Tagarira. Tendai is a shona word that means being thankful. I guess my parents were thankful to the good lord for their first son. I was given my second name,Frank after my grandfather. I am told that life was sweet in those days.

All that one had to do was to get a good education and employment would come knocking on their door step. My father had just graduated from Gweru Teachers College and got a teaching job at Mahusekwa primary school in Marondera. My father saved up money from his salary and wedding gifts and bought a white BMW Cheetah sedan. He did not want his first born traveling by public transport and he could afford the luxuries of private transport. Teaching was a lucrative career in those days and people had respect for the teaching profession,a huge contrast from today's sentiment.

(Today,Zimbabwe's hard working teachers can barely

afford a loaf of bread,but that's another story) I was born in newly independent Zimbabwe and society labeled babies like me "born frees" because we were born after independence. For a while I believed this born free theory. However,It was only a matter of time before I got a rude awakening. I should have been labeled Kurauone "born to see" because nothing in my childhood prepared me to deal with the tornado that was coming my way.

Growing up,I was protected and loved by my parents and i will forever be grateful for their unconditional love. Those days I was not aware of economics and I was not acquainted with the word inflation. Back then the Zimbabwean dollar was at par with the American dollar. Food was affordable to the majority. Our family lifestyle was a good middle class lifestyle. My father could afford taking care of the family. Once in a while he even spoiled us with holiday trips to places like Great Zimbabwe,Lake Mtirikwe and Victoria falls. Its a shame he can no longer afford such special treats for his family because the Zimbabwean crisis left him financially crippled,but he will recover,we will all recover.

(WE HAVE TO RECOVER!). In the late 80s our family moved from Marondera to Chivhu,another small town about 140km from Harare. Chivhu Town was affectionately known as Chivhu Mdara. My father got a mortgage loan and bought a house in Chivhu in a middle class neighborhood known as kumaNew Houses, where everyone seemed to know each other's business. We were neighbors to the Chiwara family and I had a kiddie crush on their little daughter,Johanna,who was about the same age as me. They was a famous song those days,Johanna give me hope and every time I heard the song play I thought of the pretty girl next door.

I also attended a lot of Sunday school,were brother Makoni taught us plays from bible stories and we performed them in church. I was a good kid and I believed what they taught us in Sunday school and church.(Today,I have one question for the good Lord,WHY?WHY? WHY?) I enrolled for grade one at Chivhu Primary School in 1989. Somehow,I landed in the same class with the pretty girl from next door. Unfortunately,I failed grade one and had to repeat it while my pretty girl went on to grade two. I was embarrassed to repeat grade one and I vowed to improve my grades.

Sometime in the 90's the Chiwara's moved to Rusape and my pretty girl was gone. It took me a while before I had another crush. In the 4th grade I found a new pretty girl and boy did I have a crush on her. Her name was Georgina and to me she was the most beautiful girl on planet earth. Unfortunately,I never mastered the courage to tell either Johanna or Georgina about the crushes I had for them. In fact,i never told anyone. However,it wasn't long before I found a new love and it wasn't a girl this time. My new love was making kites.

One time I made a big kite and the other kids in the neighborhood would run after it. They were plenty of kids in the neighborhood and we all played together. One unlucky day my famous kite was entangled on an electricity pole and I couldn't get it down. Luckily,there was a new craze in town and I joined in on the band wagon. A boy from the neighborhood named Xavier Zhakata taught me the new craft and before long I was making my own cars out of wire.

Almost every boy in the neighborhood had a car made out of wire and those who couldn't make their own cars would buy them from the Master,Xavier.

I even made me a BMW convertible and christianed it muparara denga and boy was that car beautiful. We stole the wire from the council's Garwe stadium fence to make the cars. One day we were caught stealing wires at the stadium by the council care taker,Mdara Karimapondo. He gave us the beating of a life time but that did not quell our demand for the wire. We came up with more creative ways to steal the wire. We would go to the stadium and split ourselves into two groups.

When Mdara Karimapondo was busy chasing after the one group, the second group would cut as much wire as they could with a pliers and run off in the opposite direction. I also watched a lot of television and those days we had a black and white TV. Very few families had color TV's in those days. I enjoyed cartoons,wrestling and Ezomgido,a music video show that showcased the best in Zimbabwean music. The Ezomgido show inspired us to make our own mabanchu,guitars made of fishing rope,wood planks and cooking oil gallons.

One day my father found me and my brother Donald busy making a banchu and he smashed it right in the middle and told us to go and do home work. He told us, "Zvema gitare ndezve marombe" meaning guitars are for loafers. We never attempted making a banchu again since that day. A few days later my father came home with three books,The Three Musketeers,A Tale of Two Cities and Gulliver's Travels. The books had colorful covers and beautiful pictures inside. Somehow,I found myself reading the Three

Musketeers and I enjoyed reading it.

Before long,I had completed reading Gulliver's Travels and A Tale of two Cities. As I read these books I would imagine the scenes in my mind. I would imagine being one of the three Musketeers, fighting against the evil Cardinal Richelieu or being one of the little people in Gulliver's Travels. From then on I had a love affair with literature and it is something that has stayed with me to this day. My father told me I could grow up to become anything I wanted and I was inspired. In 1996, I wrote my grade 7 and passed with flying colors.

The following year in 1997 I enrolled with St Francis of Assisi,a catholic boarding high school which was one of the finest in Mashonaland East. In boarding school I made a lot of friends and I loved athletics and beautiful girls. I was a typical teenager. If I could go back to a time in my life I would go back to high school. The day before I left for boarding school I was over the moon with excitement.

I couldn't sleep that night as I pondered what my life would be like at a catholic mission school far away from home. That night,my mother literally wrote my name on everything I was taking along in case my stuff got mixed up with other students items. On the school opening day, my father drove me to St Francis which was about an hours drive from home. St Francis of Assisi was nestled in the beautiful Nharira area,in the middle of nowhere.

The school buildings were beautiful but what stood out the most was the magnificent school church which appeared to have been carved out of pure glass. The church was indeed a sight for sore eyes. My father helped me offload my luggage and together we found a dorm,where he helped me to make my bed and unpack my stuff. Afterwards, we went to the school administration offices and my father paid my school fees.

We then said goodbye to each other and before he drove off he gave me $100.00 for pocket money. I felt like he had given me a million bucks because one hundred Zimbabwean dollars was a lot of money back then. That day, I was excited to meet other new comers. The feeling I had was indescribably beautiful. The next day, I woke up early to take a shower. I was wearing my underwear because I was not yet used to the idea of a common shower room. For some reason everyone in the shower room was calling out my name in a frenzy.

This was odd because I was just a new comer and people hardly knew my name. I only realized later that my mother had writen my name at the back of my underwear with a bold red marker. This was quite embarrassing and I had a tough time washing the ink off all my underwear. My first weeks at St Francis were exciting and I made a lot of friends. Everyday of the first week I would sleep late in the night because everyone in the dorm room had a story to tell and most of the time we talked about music and girls. I hardly studied during the first term,I was too busy trying to adjust to boarding lifestyle.

Somewhere in the middle of the term I became home sick. I longed for my mothers attention and I missed her food. I had also spend all my pocket money. I wrote a letter to my parents asking for more money and they send me a long letter with $100.00. In the letter, they told me that I had to learn how to budget my finances. From that time on I became a master at budgeting my pocket money. I was the first guy in my stream to have a girlfriend and her name was Gloria. She was a pretty lady and I couldn't help myself. Subsequently, I was a subject of dormitory gossip and somehow everyone in my stream knew who Tendai Tagarira was.

I hardly studied that term and my end of term results were devastating. On the closing day of the first school term, my father came and picked me up. He looked at my report and simply shook his head. He asked me what I thought of my performance and I was at a loss of words. I felt terrible and I knew I had to study hard the next term to prove to my father that I was serious about my studies. That was the first and last time I had bad grades. In 1998, I was in form two and part of the last stream to write ZJC examinations.

In 1998 I had already moved on to a new girlfriend.

Her name was Mable and boy was she pretty. She was in form one and every boy in my stream seemed to want her and she was mine. Everyone thought I would fail my ZJC because of my "dating escapades", but I passed with flying colors and my parents were proud of me. In form 3 I had a new girlfriend and her name was Lyndel and she was in form one. I stopped dating her in 2000 when I was in form four. In the year 2000 , I wrote my Ordinary level examinations and passed with A's and B's.

I was accepted back at St Francis for Advanced level. Unfortunately,my father could no longer afford the school fees St Francis was charging. Instead,I enrolled with a Chivhu based day school,Liebenberg High for my A-levels. The year was 2001 and I was part of the first A-level stream at Liebenberg. Since I was now living at home and attending day school I could see how my family was starting to struggle financially and I wanted to help. I even had to watch in despair when my father sold his car as he could no longer afford the high fuel prices.

Somehow,I could sense the desperation in him. Surely,this was not how he had hoped the future would turn out. My father would have wanted me to study my A-Level at St. Francis of Assisi boarding school. It must have hurt him,watching me settling in a day school whose standards were far lower than St. Francis. I was part of the first A-level stream at Liebenberg high school. I studied Accountancy,Business Studies and Geography because I planned to pursue accounting articles after A-level.

I remember applying vigorously to several Accounting firms to take me in for articles clerkship after my A-level, but all I got was a "we wish you the best in your future endeavors" response. I always worried about what would become of me after completing my A-levels, but in the meantime I had to deal with the situation at hand. For the time being I had to worry about studying and coming up with ideas of an income generating project to help my family with finances.

One day , after school I met a guy who was selling a cell phone battery. I took the guys battery,put 100% markup over what the guy wanted and sold it to the school librarian. That was my first taste of hustling and it felt good. I made a quick profit being a middle man. I reinvested the money into another venture. I bought quality silk ties which I sold to students and teachers at school for a good profit. One Friday,in the same year I went into a fuel garage kiosk to buy some biltong but there was none. It then "hit me" that I could supply this garage with biltong. I got the biltong recipe from an aunt and borrowed money from my father to buy the ingredients.

I used vinegar,black paper,coriander and salt. I bought some quality steak and cut it into thin stripes. I let the meat lie in vinegar for a while and later I applied the spices and hanged it to dry. When the biltong was ready it tasted so good. I packaged it nicely because I knew that packaging and presentation counts. I christianed the biltong,Travelers biltong. When I presented it to the fuel garage owner,she was impressed and she asked me if I could supply 300 packs every week. This was a lot and I didn't have the time nor the financial muscle to pull it off.

More so,I had to get permission from the Health

Inspector to make the biltong for commercial sales. Faced with these formidable challenges I wanted to give up but something in my gut kept telling me to proceed. After long hours of brainstorming I came up with a solution. The next day I approached a local butchery owner with an offer he couldn't refuse. Very few people can refuse a generous offer of guaranteed revenue.

I proposed a 50/50 profit sharing deal on the biltong profits to the butchery owner and he agreed. We bought the meat from his butchery and his employees prepared and packed the biltong. I collected the payments and maintained the business books. In a few weeks time I was making more money than a teacher was getting paid. My parents were proud of the entrepreneurial spirit in me. However,the Zimbabwean situation caught up with my business honeymoon and spoiled the party. After a year our sales decreased drastically. Few cars were passing through the fuel garage due to a looming nationwide fuel shortage.

Once again the progress of my life was being affected by the negative actions of the political and business architects. In November 2002 I finished my high school and on the day of my final A-level exam I sold my shareholding in the biltong business to my business partner. He was so excited and he paid me a handsome cash settlement. With that money,I bought a lot of curios and herded for the big capital,Harare where I planned to hunt for a job because I knew my father could not afford paying university studies for me. I had to make a plan to finance my further studies.

CHAPTER 3:

HARARE

"Que's for scarce commodities emerged throughout Zimbabwe. There were bread,milk and petrol Que's. Que's became the order of the day for Zimbabweans."

In Harare,I made a deal with a curio dealer at Avondale flea market. He sold my curios on his stall and we shared the profits. With that arrangement in place i dedicated more time for job hunting. For three months the soles of my shoes finished as I walked the streets of Harare in search of employment. I knocked on every company door I could find. I send my CV to many job adverts. That time I also started dating again and I met a young lady in Avondale. Her name was Tendai.

She was a city girl and she attended an elite girls school in Harare. I met her during school holidays and we hit it off. We used to watch a lot of movies at the Avondale Theater. She even baked me a chocolate cake,the sweetest treat I had ever got from any previous girlfriend. However,for some reason unknown to me to this day she stopped returning my phone calls. I walked to her brothers apartment and rang the intercom several times but noone answered. On my way back, I was socked wet by the rain. A few days later I bumped into her and she introduced me to her "new boyfriend".

I was stunned and heartbroken. From then on i stayed away from girls for a while. One day,out of the blue I got a phone call to attend a job interview at a prominent indigenous bank. That night I went on the Internet and researched about banking and the bank that had called me for the interview. The next day, I got dressed up and went for the interview. It was a group interview for a trainee money market dealership position and I was the youngest and the most unexperienced. The Chairman of the bank was part of the interview panel.

The panel grilled us for a good while and finally the

Chairman asked a question that remember clearly to this day. He asked,"So!,who do you think should succeed Mugabe?" This was an odd question for a bank Chairman to ask in a job interview. The other interviewees named guys like Simba Makoni and Morgan Tsvangirai and when it was my turn I told the Chairman what he wanted to hear . In short,I got the job. Some of you will think I am a lucky schmuck,but for me that was the beginning of a struggle,the day I got that job.

It was in April 2003. I remember it like yesterday,the excitement of getting employment when the national unemployment rate was about 60%.Money market dealers were known across H-town for their elegant dress and fancy cars and I had just landed on the gravy train. On the first day of work I work up early in the morning. As I was about to leave the house I got a phone call from a doctor at the nearby Trauma Center. He asked me to make a turn at his office immediately. He told me it was a matter of life and death.

I quickly walked there and when I arrived the doctor asked me to sit down and he delivered some very shocking news to me. Apparently,the night before,one of my close friends attempted suicide. He had overdosed on prescription pills. He even wrote a suicide note in which he named me as his best friend. He was in a bad shape and the doctor thought I could talk some sense into him. He couldn't look me in the eye because he knew he had messed up. I asked him what had pushed him to the edge but he remained silent.

To this day I don't understand why he wanted to end his life. Perhaps he was hurting from the loss of his mother who had passed away a few months before we wrote our A-level examinations in 2002. Anyway,that was how my first day at work started off. From the Trauma Center I walked quickly into town and I managed to get to work just before 8am. My first day was exciting but at the back of my mind I was worried about my friend. Weeks went by and I went through the banks training program.

I felt like I was in Peter Pan's Neverland. Unfortunately,the honeymoon didn't last for long. One day I was called into a meeting and informed that the bank no longer needed extra money market dealers because the money markets were entering the doldrums. I was given a choice,either to resign or to be put in any other department that needed manpower. Knowing too well the unemployment statistics I accepted the latter offer.

My hopes of driving a fancy car and earning a fat dealers salary were shattered and I had to deal with the reality at hand. Initially, I landed in the Back Office Department, then after a while I landed at Customer Service. After my three months probation I became a permanent employee but contrary to my probation contract I was not given any raise or benefits. I made an inquiry to the HR Department and I was advised by their secretary to keep quiet. Apparently, people who demanded their salary increase would get fired. At that point I realized that the workplace I thought was a heavenly place was actually a survival institution.

I soon learned that this bank was being ruled with an iron fist by it's Chairman. Almost all the decisions had to be made by him. The CEO and the bank directors seemed to be mere figureheads for window dressing purposes. That period was around the time when Gideon Gono was appointed the country's Reserve Bank Governor. Gono started off a famous anti corruption campaign. People thought that he was the guy who was going to clean up the mess in Zimbabwe. He had rose from a tea boy to the CEO of one of Zimbabwe's biggest banks. He was a savior in many peoples eyes.

Gono went on a massive crack down in a bid to clean up the nation's business sector. Gono's gonorrhea (as people called it) started with the crackdown of ENG Capital Pty Ltd,"affectionately known as the ENG scandal".Later,Gono's crackdown spilled over to numerous indigenous banks and other big companies. Numerous business figures fled the country fearing arrest by the new Reserve Bank Governor. Funny enough the Chairman's bank was not touched despite reports of massive irregularities withing his bank. It was rumored that he gave a massive loan to Gono to "persuade" him from shutting his bank down.

Those days were very interesting days in Zimbabwe. Gono enforced price controls for basic foodstuffs and suddenly shelves in the shops became empty. Goods started being paddled on the black market instead. Que's for scarce commodities emerged throughout Zimbabwe. There were bread,milk and petrol Que's. Que's became the order of the day for Zimbabweans. People were spending more time in Que's than at work. As if that was not enough a cash shortage also started and people had to que up to draw cash from their own bank accounts.

During the cash crisis I was in Retail Banking and suddenly people started befriending me because they wanted the cash I had access to. I was in a strategic position and the bank tellers would arrange for me enough cash that I needed. Whoever had whatever that was in short supply was making money those days. I made my small share from generous kick back's from my new friends. I was spending that money as fast as it was coming in. I registered for studies with ACCA,a top British accounting qualification and started furthering my studies by distance learning.

I moved into my own apartment in the heart of the capital. My salary was insufficient to pay my rent but the kick backs from the cash crisis venture were keeping me sustained. It wasn't long before Gono started printing huge bills of fifty thousand dollar notes and the cash crisis sought of normalized. My kick back income dried up faster than a woman's period. I started hustling to compensate my poor income. Whatever I hustled I would buy low and sell high but no matter how hard I hustled the Zimbabwean inflation beat me to the finish line. One day I went out to a birthday celebration and when i came back i was astonished when i opened my apartment door.

My furniture was gone,the bed was gone,the blankets were gone,everything was gone. Damn it,even the toilet paper was gone! I couldn't take a dump because the tissue was gone. I thought i was dreaming so i slept on the hard cold floor. Waking up the next day i realized that surely i had been robbed. I was speechless and stunned at the audacity of the crime. The selfishness of the act appalled me. That day i realized that this world is a dog eat dog world. You can have it all through hard work and honesty and yet someone can come and reap where you sowed.

What is the point of working hard then? What is the point of being a good and honest citizen when another citizen can undo all your hard work? After the robbery I decided to move into Toc-H, a boys hostel in Baines Avenue. The monthly fee to stay in the hostel was reasonable compared to the rent I was paying for my flat. The hostel provided good security, meals and laundry services. I hate cooking and laundry so Toc-H was perfect for me. I became good friends with many of the guys who stayed there. I truly enjoyed my stay at Toc-H.

It was a home away from home. That time I started dating a girlfriend who stayed at Gorge Fleming, a girls Hostel which was ten minutes away from Toc-H. One day I was coming from seeing her and I was over the moon as we had just shared our first kiss. I was walking along a pavement in total bliss. Suddenly a guy appeared from behind a tree and grabbed me by the neck. He was grabbing me so tight I couldn't breathe. I couldn't believe it. "One moment I was kissing a gorgeous girl and the next moment I was being choked to death" The guy punched me in the ribs and grabbed my cellphone.

He wanted to take my trousers and shoes as well but luckily a car drove by and he ran away. That car probably saved my life. When I got to Toc-H I notified my friends about the incident and they told me,"Welcome to the Avenues". Apparently,a lot of muggings were taking place around the area I had been robbed. Other Toc-H residents had also been robed in a similar fashion behind the same tree. We all decided to set a trap for that guy. We caught him and we beat the criminal out of him. To my knowledge that was the last time anyone was mugged behind that tree. As for my stolen cell phone, I never recovered it. (Mid2004)For a while I worked in Retail Banking then by some stroke of luck I landed in the Treasury and Finance department.

I made it a point to gain as much experience and exposure as I could. By this time the Zimbabwean inflation had reduced our salaries to mere peanuts so a meeting of all non managerial staff was called for. In this meeting it was decided that a new, fresh workers committee for the bank be established and somehow my name came up for nomination. I have no idea who nominated me or why? I was voted the deputy president for the bank's workers committee sometime in early 2004. Little did i realize what a negative effect this would have on my life the next few months. We set up meetings with management to negotiate a pay increase and boy I was excited! I love to debate and negotiate. I love the trill of it. We negotiated for the bank to pay half of the staffs lunch fees at the canteen. We negotiated for transportation and overtime pay for those who had to work overtime.

We successfully negotiated for the return of some employees who were on suspension. It felt good. I felt like i was doing humanitarian work by lobbying to improve working conditions for overall non managerial employees. However,we were still deadlocked with management over what percentage salary increase non managerial employees would get. One day the Chairman called me to his office and I was excited to meet the big man.

He asked me why i was lobbying for a salary increase for the employees. Being naive,I thought his question was sincere so I explained to him about the rising cost of living and the astronomical inflation that had reduced the value of our salaries. As I spoke he was constantly nodding his head. Suddenly,he stood up,opened his office window and asked me to look outside. I will never forget the words that came out of his mouth. He said,"Young man, do you see that building next door,Its empty,no one is renting it. Why don't you open your own bank there and pay your employees that salary you want me to pay. This is my bank! Get out of my office" I was stunned beyond words and i left his office as ordered by him. That moment i realized that he who has the gold makes the rules.

That day , i resolved that i would also go for gold in life,that way i would never have anyone setting a cap on what and how much i can achieve in life. Out of curiosity I asked some people how the big man had come to own his own bank. I did research and i found out that this man was born poor indeed. He got a scholarship to study economics somewhere in India. After the liberation struggle he and other now famous Zimbabwe businessman are said to have siphoned a black empowerment grand and shared it amongst themselves. I was amazed.

Chapter 4

BOTSWANA AND BACK.

"Nevertheless,the prospect of getting out of Zimbabwe outweighed any risk factor of the unknown."

I was fed up with everything,the job,the constructive frustration from management and the Zimbabwean free fall economy. I was fed up! In April,2005 I quit my job,got part of my severance pay,packed my bags and decided to herd for neighboring Botswana in search for greener pastures. There were many stories of people who got high paying jobs in Botswana with their Zimbabwean qualifications. I would have liked to go to London,but Britain had imposed stringent travel and visa regulations on Zimbabweans.

Besides,I couldn't even afford a plane ticket to London. My other easy option was South Africa but the tales of crime and violence made me grinch. So Botswana it was. I had 500 pulas and I knew it was not enough. Nevertheless,the prospect of getting out of Zimbabwe outweighed any risk factor of the unknown. I booked my train ticket from Harare to Bulawayo. The train was dirty and filthy regardless of the fact that I was traveling in first class. That is how bad the service of National Railways of Zimbabwe had become.

From Bulawayo,i boarded a minibus all the way to the Botswana Border Post. I applied for 90 days stay in Botswana but the immigration official stamped 30 days on my passport and gave it back to me with a sinister grin on her face. It didn't occur to me that many Tswana immigration officials were not particularly fond of Zimbabweans. Their arrogance towards Zimbabweans was unbelievable. From Francis town i boarded the night train to Gaborone,Botswana's capital. I was excited and scared all at the same time but i carried on with the pursuit of my dreams. I arrived in Gaborone early in the morning and i got off at the train station. It then hit me. What was i thinking? where did I think I was going?

In that moment,I remembered i had the phone number of a guy in Gaborone. His young brother used to call him on my cell phone. I bought a sim card and phoned the guy. I lied to him that i was supposed to meet someone at the train station,but they had not turned up. He gave me directions to his flat in Broadhurst and that's how i got accommodation during my stay in Botswana. Through this guy,i met some very good people also from Zimbabwe, who were working in Gaborone.

One of these people that I became close friends with was Tindo. People called him Dred Jerry and he treated me like his own brother. He was a humble Rastafarian and he lived a simple but happy life. Everyday,I would wake up and walk into town looking for employment , but i soon learned that it was difficult finding a job in Botswana. In fact,to me it was easier to land a man on the moon than getting a job in Gaborone. Many Batswana's I came across did not like Zimbabweans. Truly speaking many of them hated our guts.

Their arrogance and xenophobic hatred was unbelievable. It was worse than racism. I realized that there was no way I was ever going to get a job despite my belief in miracles. I was also becoming an economic burden to my new found friends, who had offered me accommodation and food. One day i humbly accepted the sad reality of my situation despite my high expectations. I was out of luck.(July 2005) I packed my small bag and hit the road back to agony.

The journey back to Zimbabwe felt long and hard because i knew the economic situation was only getting worse. Life in Zimbabwe was a constant daily struggle to survive and I hated it. Why should I suffer in the land of my forefathers? Anyway,i was back home at my mothers house with nothing but my bag of clothes and a sad story of my experiences in Botswana. My parents were happy to see me and I comforted myself in their love. Days went by and i didn't bother getting out of the house.

I was angry at life,i was angry with my situation and i wanted to change it. Seeing my looming depression,my father asked me to join him in a little business venture he was pursuing,while i figured out my life. The business venture was buying and selling cattle. I financed the project with the little money I had saved up from my severance pay. We started the business and we did all right. Our profit margins were good but the Zimbabwean inflation was constantly eroding our buying power.

One day, I decided to give the diaspora another shot. I did not tell anyone my exact plan. I asked my young brother Donald in a hypothetical scenario and he told me bluntly,wakumhanya bani,tjoka ita steady "dude, you are going mad crazy, you need to calm down". Nevertheless,I continued conjuring up my plan. I would look at the maps of the world and imagine life in another country. It had to be better than Zimbabwe.

Even Iraq was a better prospect for me at the time.

With a good salary i would have become

Alqueda,that's how desperate i was.

CHAPTER5:

NAMIBIA

"By this time i only had R20.00 in my pocket, yep R20.00 and hope"

In December 2005 i went on the Internet and found myself goggling Namibia. What popped up was something about a town called Walvisbay. It caught my attention,wow!the pictures,my god!,beautiful! Walvisbay,the article said,is the fishing and import hub of Namibia with a population of about 50,000 people. Something in my mind told me this was it,the place i needed to go to. Within a week, I phoned the bus that was traveling to Namibia and inquired the bus fare.

It was about R300.00. I packed my bag,changed my Zim dollars on the black market and got me about R500.00. When I got to the bus station they told me it was fully booked. I bribed the bus captain for a seat and out of the blue there was now a vacant seat available for me in the bus. "Talk about being ripped off by a bus captain!" I boded the bus and in no time we were driving off to Namibia,where i intended to make my way to the coastal town of Walvisbay. After paying the bus fare and the bribe I had R150.00 left. I inquired from a young Namibian pastor who was seating next to me the cost of a bus to Walvisbay. He told me that i would need R100.00.

Being an accountant, i did the math's in my head and realized i only had R50.00 left in my budget. In Namibia R50.00 can buy you lunch in a cheap restaurant. I started wondering what i would do when i got to Walvisbay with a paltry R50.00 in my pocket. Thinking back about it i was either crazy or crazy. Damn it! I was crazy. The young pastor asked me why I was traveling to Walvisbay. I told him I was running away from the economic problems in Zimbabwe. He told me that one day Zimbabwe would improve but it was too late for anyone to talk me into reversing my decision. I had made up my mind,only fate would decide how my life was going to turn out. There was no way I was going to sit around and wait for Zimbabwe to improve.

I had to improve myself,I had to get away from the madness. I wasn't coping well with the economic pressure in Zimbabwe. If I had stayed in Zimbabwe with the HIGH level of stress I had, I would have become crazy,literally. I needed a change of environment and I was taking a chance. I was prepared to sleep in the park and to push a broom and work my way up. (Dec, 2005) We arrived at the Namibian Rundu border post and I could smell a breath of fresh air.

There,i met a gentleman who was also traveling to Walvisbay. His name was Langton. He told me that he had found a job there. His soon to be employer had financed his travel fares and would provide him with accommodation as well. He was a tailor and his soon to be employer had a small clothing shop in Walvisbay. He was excited about starting his new job as it would enable him to earn some foreign currency which he planned to use to feed his family back home. Little did i know that through Langton I would find my initial accommodation in the coastal town of Walvisbay.

We talked about the political situation in Zimbabwe and we all hoped for a fruitful start in Walvisbay. The bus arrived in Namibia's capital,Windhoek just after midnight and we had to sleep in the bus until the next morning. In the morning , we asked for directions to the Walvisbay taxi rank and after a long walk we found it. There was a minibus already half full and we took the back seat. I bought some food for thirty dollars and shared it with Langton. Within a few minutes the minibus was full and we were driving off to Walvisbay.

It was a cold Sunday morning. For about an hour we both sat in the bus and stared at the scenery outside without saying a word to each other. I guess we were both pondering of our new beginning so far away from home. By this time i only had R20.00 in my pocket, yep!, R20.00 and hope. After about a four hour drive we finally arrived in Walvisbay,a lovely town,sandwiched between the Kalahari desert and the Atlantic ocean. The words,"Welcome to Walvisbay,an oasis of opportunities" greeted us from a nicely crafted road sign.

Finally,i had reached my destination and it was worth it. I felt a certain calmness in my heart. I took a deep breath and said a little prayer in my head. We got off at a service station. The air was moist and cool. We looked for a telephone booth and Langton made a phone call to his employer. He was given directions to a church function the employer was attending at the Walvisbay municipality hall ,which was just a stone throw away from the service station. We waited outside the hall for Langton's employer. Langton asked me what my plan was since his employer was expecting only himself.

I told him i would ask his employer where i could find cheap accommodation and then leave. After a few minutes his employer came out. He introduced himself and his wife as Martin and Benedert. They were a lovely,happy and friendly couple. I explained to them my situation and that I was looking for cheap accommodation and they invited me to join them for lunch at their house. That lunch was the first decent meal i had since leaving Zimbabwe. Over lunch,we discussed everything from Zimbabwean politics and the free fall Zimbabwean economy. Finally,after a long discussion they told me I could sleep at their shop for the night and they were kind enough to give me a sleeping bag.

At their clothing shop we met another Zimbabwean who was also working for Martin and Benedert. He was staying and sleeping at the back of the shop. He was an elderly man and his name was Mutero. He was a nice man. He was glad we brought him company. That day, we slept late in the night discussing our Zimbabwean plight. I slept on the floor inside the sleeping bag and i was happy. I had a roof over my head, well at least for the night. The next day we woke up early.

We took turns bathing in a small plastic bucket. We

had a small breakfast of dry bread and hot black tea. The old man,Mutero,packed two slices of bread for me in a small lunch bag. He told me i would need it for strength when i walked around the town looking for employment. I asked him to keep my traveling bag for me as i planned to come and collect it when i found accommodation. Little did i realize how naive i was. The unemployment rate in Namibia was about 40%.Walvisbay is a predominantly Afrikaans speaking town and to this day I haven't mastered the enthusiasm to speak the language.

I knocked on every employers door that I came across but i got an all too familiar response,Gern Werk!, Afrikaans for NO WORK!. Realizing my now complex situation i decided to walk to the Walvisbay lagoon to clear my thoughts. I followed the road signs. On my way there i noticed a golf course and i decided to check it out. When i got there a Boer guy asked me if i was a caddy. To this day I still wonder why he thought of me as a caddy. His assumption didn't go down very well with me.

Being strapped for cash and desperate I carried his golf bag throughout his nine hole session. He paid me R100.00 for my back breaking labor. I went back to the clothing shop and explained to Langton and Mutero my experiences. They related with my situation and asked Martin and his wife if i could stay with them until my situation got better. I will forever be grateful to their gracious gesture that day. I shared my golf caddying earnings with them and we pooled our funds and bought some food.

The next few weeks i would repeat the same routine,wake up in the morning, walk around Walvisbay looking for a job,go the golf course and offer my caddying services to the wealthy golfers. Other times i didn't get any caddying gigs,some days i did , but at least i was contributing towards the food bill. One day i was watching the wealthy golfers getting out of their luxury cars and i thought to myself, "I should be that guy who is playing golf,not the caddy" There i was with my excellent accounting qualifications,my banking experience and i was caddying for wealthy golfers,what a shit pit I was in. Some days I helped the guys at the shop. I would sweep,take out the garbage and do anything I could do to help out.

I became good friends with Martin and a few times he would invite me to his house for red wine and music. We had similar tastes in music,we both liked The Temptations,Berry White and Marvin Gaye. Martin told me about his childhood and he related to my situation as he had also migrated to Namibia from South Africa when he was a young boy. Both of us had a fantasy of living a happy and simple life on a Caribbean Island,far away from the worries of the world. Martin was indeed my first Namibian friend. Those were some of the happy moments, but they didn't last for long.

No matter how much red wine I drank the reality of my situation was always waiting for me to sober up. One day,early in the morning i went into a college with my CV looking for a job as i did with many companies. The receptionist greeted me nicely in english and not in the usual afrikaans. I explained to her that i was prepared to offer accounting lectures if they ever needed a lecturer. Fortunately for me,they were desperately looking for a lecturer for their accounting courses.

I couldn't believe my luck. She took my CV and asked me to come back in an hour when the branch administrator was in. I came back after thirty minutes and waited for my appointment. The branch administrator came in and she invited me into her office, introducing herself as Nanette Sigh. She went through my CV and told me it was impressive. They needed a lecturer for their finance classes starting January the next year. She told me that it would be a part time job and that i had to get my own work visa, in oder to get the job.

I paid a small fortune to an immigration agency and i got the work visa. Within a few days it was Christmas and it was the most hopeful Xmas i have ever had. I was happy and excited of my new employment opportunity , even though I had no idea how much the job would pay me. "I should have asked how much the job paid,i should have asked!" January came and i started work. I was paid on an hourly basis and the rate was ridiculous. My God!,that college was really chizzling me and paying me peanuts. To them I was cheap immigrant labor force. Even a cleaner would have refused that paltry amount the college called my salary,but what could I do? I was desperate and at least the job allowed me to make use of my intellect. I moved out of the shop and started renting a tiny unused car garage for accommodation. My only property were my clothes and a   small bag.

CHAPTER 6

FALSE HOPE

"While the politicians fought over ministry allocations,the people were dying. The people's confidence needed a resurection and what seemed to be their only hope was turning into a childish squabble."

One day while i was researching for a lecture at a local library i met a well dressed gentlemen who told me he was also from Zimbabwe. He was an MBA graduate and former lecturer for a prominent university in Zimbabwe. He was busy setting up a training company with two other partners,a Zambian and a Namibian. I told him i was good with finance and accounting and he arranged a meeting for me with his partners.

They explained to me their ambitious project and asked me to come on board since they needed someone with a good finance background. I accepted. Here was an opportunity for me to be part of a business. The Zambian and the Namibian provided the start up finance and we,the Zimbabweans, would use our intellect to design training modules and facilitate the training seminars.

Our first training seminar,which I developed and facilitated, made us a good sum of money as we had a good attendance. It was the biggest amount of money I had ever made in two days. As the money rolled in i started to notice the true colors of my business partners. Believe me,money reveals a mans true colors. Some of the business partners wanted us to split the profit and share it immediately. We didn't even pay our office rent yet and some partners were already discussing profit sharing.

I wanted to invest the money into the business even though I was desperate for cash. (January 2007) As you might have guessed our business partnership did not succeed because of our different goals. To make it worse,one of the business partner's brother's apartment was robbed and they wanted me to take the fall. I was their prime suspect. Talk about being a defenseless immigrant in a foreign land. I told them I would not pay them anything and to this day,I have kept my word.

Why should I pay for things I did not steal? They threatened to have me deported and I told them to go ahead and try it. They were jealous of me because i had started out my own training and consulting business. They thought they owned me and they could not stomach to see me going solo and doing well for myself. I quietly hired a lawyer in case these goons tried anything. Those goons could go to hell for all i cared.

Selfish greedy bastards! From that day on I resolved to start and run my own business ventures. I didn't realize that this dream has its fair share of problems. By this time i had moved into a decent lodge and i had acquired my own office equipment. I wanted to advertise my business in the newspaper and i didn't want to spend too much money doing it, so approached the newspaper and asked them if i could write articles for small businesses. They agreed. At the bottom of each article i put my contact details and soon i started getting clients.

Some wanted business plans, others wanted training and i provided all the services i could. One day i went to the newspaper offices to submit my articles for the week. The receptionist told me that the editor wanted to see me. I thought that finally my work was being noticed and appreciated by the editor but i was dead wrong. When I got in his office i held out my hand to greet him but the man did not greet me back. He did not even offer me a seat. Instead, he started quizzing me about who had given me the permission to write in "his" newspaper. I was offended.

A hairy white man giving me the third degree attitude! What a cheek! I asked him not to insult my intelligence and to behave humanly before we could discuss anything. He told me his name and i remembered something i had brushed off a few days before. It was the same white man who had made racist remarks to the lady who answered my phone. I was not going to suck up to him just because he was a white man. I don't suck up to anyone,not even a black man.

I soon learned that this man was just an employee and that in fact, a black man owned the newspaper. I wrote a long letter to the owner expressing my disgust in his editor's behavior. The newspaper owner set up a meeting with me and his editor to arbitrate the fuming dispute. We made the peace but to this day i never forgave that rude bastard of an editor and I make no apologies for my words. I stopped writing for them and I started writing for another newspaper altogether.

I also started writing my first book which is titled,Beyond Money. registered a publishing company and saved up money for print. I sold a couple of copies by direct marketing but not enough to break even. To this day,a huge pile of unsold copies stands in my flat and I give most away for free. I am however proud of myself for publishing the book. I am still looking for avenues to market and sell my books and I will not stop searching because I believe people have a right to read them.

Meanwhile,I continue to write about things that are dear to me. Right now i have tried a lot of things in life. I just want to see one project of mine grow into a sustainable business. I want to make a living doing what i love and right now i love online and print publishing. I do not want to look for a job that I am not passionate about. Life is too short,why should I waste it pursuing things I am not passionate about? Then again,I have to do whatever i have to in order to help out my family back home in Zimbabwe. I don't like to discuss Zimbabwean politics but Goddamn it! Our political situation affects me deeply.

First there was political violence,shady elections then Thabo Mbeki says "Crisis,What crisis in Zimbabwe?" What did he mean? I would love to be in my country enjoying peace and economic prosperity, but there is too much corruption and violence. In Zimbabwe,I am considered a "born free",I was born after the war so I am considered politically immature to express my opinion,but I will express my opinion. I will not be made to be silent while I witness terrible injustices being done to fellow human beings. I will fight with my paper and pen.

I hate the fact that corrupt politicians and corrupt businessman have been allowed to run the country to the ground. I hate that the world watches the situation in Zimbabwe like a football match. I hate that we have a Central Bank that practices voodoo economics in order to appease the political masters. I hate the fact that politics has messed up business,health and social services. I hate that hospitals have to send away dying people because of the unavailability of medication. I hate that the government has failed to retain Zimbabwean professionals.

The other day, I was excited when the Zimbabwean "deal" was signed. I thought finally, a political settlement that will allow us to go back home and rebuild the nation's economy. I even had investors willing to back up a magazine publication I plan on launching in Zimbabwe. I was excited. The investors were excited. A stable Zimbabwe is a good business market. The investor was about to transfer the funds for the magazine then the news came out; our politicians let me down again. They were failing to agree on the sharing of ministries so they let the whole nation suffer.

I was disappointed beyond measure. While the politicians fought over ministry allocations,the people were dying. The people's confidence needed a resurrection and what seemed to be their only hope was turning into a childish squabble. Our inflation was at 230,000,000.00%. My God! In South Africa,they set alight,maimed and killed Zimbabwean immigrants. They call us Amakwerekwere,a derogatory term referring to foreigners.

They say we are taking their jobs. I think they misdirected their frustration to a weaker and vulnerable group that is not protected in their constitution. The resentment for foreigners by some black South Africans is amazing. A day will come when the South African people will realize how much they benefited from the Zimbabwean economic crisis. Lets face it,business was booming in South Africa because of the increased demand for their goods and services by Zimbabweans.

Zimbabweans were importing almost everything from South Africa, yet they call those very consumers Amakwerekwere. What happened to ubuntu? What happened to humanity? Didn't Zimbabwe take care of political exiles from South Africa during their apartheid era? Did Zimbabwe not help to fight apartheid in South Africa? Why torture,maim and kill a starving desperate and defenseless neighbor? When your neighbor is in trouble, do you not help him? Instead, you pursue quiet diplomacy. Quiet diplomacy my ass! The xenophobic violence that erupted in South Africa appalled me.

I do not hate South Africans, but it hurt me badly when I saw images of our brothers being chased,beaten and set alight. I hope one day there will be a Truth and Healing Commission set up to heal the wounds of tortured immigrants in South Africa. What happened to Zimbabwe might easily happen anywhere in Africa. Let us not allow political differences to drag us to hell. We will never agree on everything. Its just human nature.

Let us learn to disagree honorably, Let us learn to give others a chance. Let us learn to respect the will of the people. Let us embrace democracy, freedom of speech and ideas. Let us learn to tolerate one another despite of our differences in race,nationality,tribe,sex and social standing. It is the only way we can move forward and built a better Africa,a better Zimbabwe, a better world.

CHAPTER 7 :

LAMENTATIONS

"Maybe one day i will look back at this book and realize i was blowing things out of proportion,but right now this is exactly how i feel. I am angry,I am pissed off and i am disappointed. In fact, I am mad as hell!"

Many times I feel like it's just me against the world but I am not going to give up. I will fight till the day i die. I will fight with my words and my pen. Maybe one day i will look back at this book and realize i was blowing things out of proportion,but right now this is exactly how i feel. I am angry,I am pissed off and i am disappointed. In fact,I am mad as hell! A couple of months ago i approached a certain entrepreneur and convinced him to partner with me on a business project i had in mind.

I did not ask him to bankroll me with money,only office space and office equipment to make the business look respectable. He agreed. We started the project with much enthusiasm. I got a friend to design some business cards and letterheads for the company. I got our website up and running and started marketing the business but i later realized i made one critical mistake. I included my Shona surname on the business contact forms.

A "white" friend later told me in confidence that in Namibia, having a name that doesn't sound white can cost you big business in certain circles despite the brilliance of your business ideas. I was stunned and disappointed. In this year of 2008,racism is still rife in Namibia,in the month America elected its first black president,Barrack Obama. In Walvisbay , its called silent racism. The blacks seem to know their place and the whites certainly know their place.

I seem to be one of the few who doesn't know his place,well according to some assholes!.One time,i happened to visit a famous town in the northern part of Namibia. To be honest it was the least of places i expected to experience first hand racism. I went into a certain Toyota dealership to check out the cars and i had to use the toilet. I asked one employee for the directions and what he told me amazed me to this day. He told me i had to use the toilet for the blacks and not the one for the whites.

I could not believe it , in 2008,in Namibia,certain toilets are still segregated on racial lines. In open defiance I used the one for the so called whites. I asked to see the manager to explain this racial gibberish about the toilet arrangement in their company. He failed to explain himself. I told him that in my country, we don't tolerate such nonsense. I was pissed off to the bone. I don't like racists. They are ignorant and arrogant bastards who think they are superior to everyone else.

Why does race matter at all? Why should someone judge me by the color of my skin and not the content of my character? Racists are cowards with an inferior complex. They feel good when they undermine other people. They enslaved us and colonized us for what? They interfered in our ways and we lost our sacred culture as a result. We had a fully functional Zimbabwean economy long before the racists came. We had peace and order. We did not judge anyone by the color of their skin.

We did not consume our lives with the pursuit of worldly goods and possessions. We valued relationships,we had respect for each other,we had respect for the environment,then along came the racists. They stole our cattle and they took our land. They moved us into dry arid areas. They told us we needed permits to walk our own lands. They forced us to pay taxes. We had to fight back for our country. We lost many brothers and sisters in that fight but in the end we triumphed.

After independence many of our elected politicians started fattening their pockets and soon forgot about the people. They were seduced by the adulterous prostitute of materialism. They forgot the will of the people and felt threatened by the people. They started suppressing the peoples voice,much to the annoyance of Zimbabwe's ghosts. The whole nation was plunged into chaos. Sons and daughters were scattered beyond the borders. Husbands had to leave their wives. Children had to leave their parents.

Wives had to leave their families to go and forage in foreign lands for the upkeep of their families. However,at our breaking point, we found hope again but it's a fragile hope and we must handle it with care. We must learn from our old ways about sustainable growth. We must embrace our history and learn from it. Our ancestors were successful people long before the white man came to Zimbabwe. We made do with organic farming. Our produce was healthy and it was not genetically modified.

At times I imagine what life would have been like if the Westerners had not interfered in our ways. I wonder what Zimbabwe would have been like had we not been colonized. I truly wonder. Our old ways were sustainable to the environment. We were not driven by materialism and greed. We lived a simple and happy life. Today the world is mourning about global warming. Our ancestors knew long before how to avoid such catastrophes by living in harmony with their environment.

CHAPTER 8

DRIFTING ON THIN ICE

When judgment day comes as taught in the bible I
hope the suffering Zimbabweans get an exemption
and go to haven."

(Sunday, Nov 23, 2008), Today my brother Donald phoned me from Zimbabwe. He is desperate and disappointed with the economic situation. We decided to pursue a certain deal that might help alleviate the cash situation back home and possibly improve our financial situation as a family. The deal requires courage and accuracy. It's a risky deal and im putting my neck on the line. I also spoke to my father and he told me that at least the family was coping. They planted their own maize at the farm and they are looking forward to a good harvest in 2009.

I hope the rains will come for the peoples sake. However,I worry about the effect of global warming on Zimbabwe's weather pattern. The people responsible for commissioning such studies are busy fighting over ministry allocations. Its a known fact that global warming is affecting weather patterns.

Many of our farmers continue using methods of planting that are probably incompatible with the new weather pattern. For my fathers sake and for the nations sake I hope and pray that it rains. My father told me that the look on people's faces is a sad, terrible and hungry look.

He said people have grown skinny and their faces have no sign of life. He told me he does not know how long the situation in the country will last because at this point people have run out of hope and patience. I could only say to him, "Our government has let us down, it has let the people down!". He comforted me and told me that someday things will change for the better. I hope he is right. Personally,I have no hope left. I have little confidence in our politicians of either political party. They seem to be greedy and insensitive to the peoples needs.

At this stage, i start thinking of the lessons of Sunday school when i was a kid. We were taught that the good Lord takes care of his people during a crisis. I respect and fear God but sometimes I wonder if Zimbabwe is on his agenda. Why should innocent people die and corrupt power greedy politicians live long? A friend told me that his aunt died recently. She died sitting on a chair. She simply closed her eyes,never to open them again.

I wonder if she died of grief and sadness. Maybe she lost all the hope she once had,wondering Why?, How? but she was too tired and hungry to answer these questions so she closed her eyes and passed on in silence. Why cant the power hungry politicians pass on in silence? Is life fair at all? Someone once joked that a Zimbabwean politician died, so did an American and a British politician.

They all went to hell for their deeds. In hell, they were allowed one phone call to their respective countries per year. The American went to the phone booth and before he even finished his greetings with the other side, his usd$500 was finished. He could not believe how expensive a call from hell to America cost, it was ridiculously expensive. The Brit also went to the pay phone and phoned his home country. Within a few seconds, his 400 pounds ran out. 'Bloody expensive!', he screamed out.

Finally, it was the Zimba's turn. The American and the Brit wondered how long he was going to talk since the Zimbabwean dollar had lost its value by 230,000,000%. However, the Zimbabwean spoke for hours for just one Zimbabwean dollar. The Brit and the American were speechless and stunned. How could it be possible? They lodged a complaint to the devil about the matter. The devil laughed and simply told them,"Gentlemen, relax, he was making a local call from one hell to another that's why it was so cheap".

This stupid joke gets me thinking. Is Zimbabwe that bad? Are we really a living hell? If that's the case then when judgment day comes as taught in the bible, I hope the suffering Zimbabweans get an exemption and go to haven. In fact,i am praying right now. "Dear God, i am not praying for myself right now. I am praying for my people who are suffering at the hands of a tyrant government and heartless politicians. I am praying that you take the lives of the corrupt politicians.

I am praying that you fill the peoples hearts with courage to revolt against the beast. Send us Moses to deliver us from our oppressors and lead us to the promised land. The land is red with the blood of innocent political violence victims. The people are hungry and have nowhere to turn. I am turning to you lord. Provide for your people, free them from the oppressor, renew their lives again. Show us that you are the mighty and powerful God that we serve. I am asking for a miracle oh lord.

No man can solve the problems in Zimbabwe. Only you can. Save us oh lord. I am praying for a miracle. Deliver us from the evil that resides in the hearts of our corrupt politicians. You are our only hope. We need a miracle oh lord. I beg you, in Jesus name. AMEN". These days when i meet people they just shake their heads and say, "brother your country is fucked!".

They read what's going on in Zimbabwe and they feel sorry for me. I don't want their sympathy but they always make a funny comment whenever they see me. Are we the sorriest people on earth right now? It hurts me badly to suffer because of political turmoil. In December 2008,I met an old friend and he told me what he had been up to in Zimbabwe. He told me that at one point he was so broke,desperate and circumstances forced him to operate an escort agency. He hired some upmarket prostitutes and he would organize rich clients for them.

He told me the clients were paying for the sexual services in hard currency,mainly US dollars. I can't judge him because I know the situation in Zimbabwe. Should the situation ever improve I hope the new government will set up a Healing Commission to heal the hearts of traumatized Zimbabweans. We are a traumatized society in need of mental therapy. I definitely need to see a shrink myself, but I cant afford one at the moment. Funny enough,i read on the news online that some guy was caught with 215 million US dollars trying to cross the Mozambican border into Zimbabwe.

215 million US dollars! in cash! Something is definitely going on in Zimbabwe. There are people who are profiting immensely from this ongoing crisis. The central bank in Zimbabwe dosent even have that kind of money according to press reports but some guy is driving around with 215 million USD cash in the boot of his car. It beats all logic,but hey, that is Zimbabwe for you. There is a disease growing in Zimbabwe.

It is an epidemic of greed and profiteering. Everyone wants to get rich quickly in Zimbabwe. You just need to look at the ridiculous charges of goods and services. The government should accept that their Zimbabwean dollar is dead. Nobody wants it. I don't even want to see it. The government should make a plan to simply liberalize the economy and allow the use of foreign currency. They should allow trade to be done in any other currency except the Zimbabwean dollar. In fact, everyone should be paid and transact in forex. It's the only way out of this mess.

A resurrection of the Zimbabwean dollar is not feasible after what they did to it. They should let the Zimbabwean dollar rest in peace. Gideon Gono should preside over it's burial because he is largely responsible for it's death. After the funeral service of the Zimbabwean dollar,Gono should have the decency to go and hang himself on the rope of shame. It's the only honorable thing he can do for the people of Zimbabwe. History will judge him harshly. Never has there been a kiss ass Reserve Bank Governor. Gono betrayed the nation.

CHAPTER 9:

TRYING TO MAKE SENSE OF IT.

"We,Zimbabweans,should help and uplift each other irregardless of social standing or political affiliation."

I have been thinking hard lately. I am thinking about the whole Mugabe phenomenon. The old man certainly did some good things all right. He implemented one of Africa's greatest education policies and the educated Zimbabwean nation is a testimony of that vision. I am told that in 1995,Zimbabwe had a higher literacy rate compared to USA. Mugabe also freed our minds from fear of the white man. Largely,because of him,Zimbabweans see themselves as equals with any race. Fear of the white man is still dominant in much of African countries and in Zimbabwe it is no longer there. However,Mugabe should be careful not to reverse his greatest legacy which is education in my opinion.

His government should make a concrete plan to ensure that teachers get paid and schools resume the most important task of educating the young generation who will one day be the leaders of Zimbabwe. Once, in Botswana I was saddened beyond words when I met a qualified Zimbabwean teacher who had resorted to vending bananas and oranges on a taxi rank in Gaborone.

I didn't have to ask him why he was vending vegetables alongside taxi rank hooligans. I understood his situation and I could feel his pain. There was a sense of hopelessness and frustration when we discussed our Zimbabwean situation. The man simply shook his head and said Politics imhata, "Politics is an asshole!" This is what the Zimbabwean crisis has reduced our teachers to, vegetable toting vender's. "Who is going to teach Zimbabwe's children then?",I asked the man. "The bloody politician!s",he replied. Unfortunately,the affluent politicians send their children to study overseas while the children of the masses are left to become illiterate. When I was in high school there were several of these "politicians" children.

I remember once when me,Chris and other guys stole bread from the dining room. We were caught by the Boarding Master and he send us to the school principal,who was a no nonsense man. It was very clear we were all going to get the beating of a life time. Funny enough,Chris "the politicians child", was summoned alone into the principals office for some "counseling", after which he was send off to the classroom. As for us,the children of non politicians,we were given the beating of a life time in the principals office. He even had the audacity to make us choose the whips of our choice as he had an assortment of them in a drawer.

He even had names for these whips. We got the beating of a life time that day, a well deserved beating and we were pissed off to the bone because Chris did not get a beating since he was the son of an affluent politician. Justice does not discriminate but that day I realized that there is also Selective Justice and boy does it discriminate. Yep!,im starting the new year of 2009 broke and up to my neck in debts and I have no idea how I am going to pay them.

Somehow, I will have to figure it out. The huge chunk of my debt I owe it to my lawyer for divorce proceedings, yep I said it,"divorce proceedings". You see,I was never really married,I was technically married. This is what happened. Once,in mid 2006 I was frustrated since I could not secure a visa to the Cayman Islands because of my Zimbabwean passport which is hard to travel anywhere with. I met this one foreign lady and I explained to her my situation in a conversation.

She gave me what appeared like a straightforward solution to my problem. She asked me to marry her,that way the Cayman Islands would hopefully approve my visa to travel and work there. She asked me to pay her a hefty sum and then she took me to court and married me just like that. God Dam it I was desperate. Her offer seemed like a good idea at the time. I did not have a serious girlfriend and I just wanted to leave the African continent. Funny enough only a couple of weeks after my "marriage" I met a woman that I truly love. When I met her I realized that I had to cancel my "marriage" so I hired a lawyer and got a divorce.

The lawyer charged me a hefty fee but it was worth it, well, i hope it was worth it. Right now,I have resorted to wheeling and dealing. It's risky a business but what can I do? Maybe one day I wont have to wheal and deal for a living. All I want in this life is to setup sustainable enterprises that create opportunities and employment for other people.

I also want to get heavily involved in philanthropy,in oder to give back to the poor and needy. Once,I read an article about a family in Zimbabwe that resorted to eating an old skin hide of a cow that died 10 years ago. I have to admit,that is the sorriest thing I have ever read. The article said that the family boiled the skin hide for long hours to make it soft. They scraped off it's furs and bon apetie!. Even a wild dog wont eat the skin of a dead animal. Not even the vulture would eat it.

Is there any justice in this world? Whats next when the skin hide gets finished? Are they going to start eating one another like hyenas? Its big a shame. We,Zimbabweans should help and uplift each other irregardless of social standing or political affiliation.

In the spirit of love for Zimbabwe our politicians should forget their past grievance's and start working together in harmony. What kind of nation are we turning into if a man has to eat a ten year old skin hide? What good is in having SUV driving,flamboyant politicians when the masses are eating cow hides for survival?

What good is in giving only the politically connected opportunities? This is a social decay in Zimbabwe. The political wealthy Zimbabweans want to keep all the nations wealth for themselves. It seems only the "politically connected" can do big business and become wealthy in Zimbabwe. This "who do you know" attitude needs to end. What good is in driving a fancy car when your neighbor is starving to death because you bought that car by hording everything and creating an artificial shortage in the market? What good is in ripping each other off?

The gap between the wealthy minority and the poor majority in Zimbabwe is unbelievable and unjustified. The politicians are breeding a very angry generation because of their actions. What chance is there for the new generation Zimbabwean? I wonder what my chance for success in Zimbabwe is. Will my hard work suffice or will i need to pay homage to the minority in oder to get by in my own country? I wonder?

Did we defeat the white minority only to be replaced by a black minority? You don't need to go far to notice Zimbabwe's rich minority. They usually stay in the well manicured neighborhoods of Harare,affectionately known as "kumaDales". They have elaborate villas and drive cars that make a statement,"I am rich and I want you to see it",literally. You find these high society brothers and sisters in the posh establishments of Zimbabwe.

How they made their wealth is a debatable subject because no one remembers them ever working hard to achieve that status. It seems as if by some strange stroke of magic they became rich almost overnight. Frankly,I have nothing against being wealthy. I am not a Communist but ill gotten wealth is a dangerous cancer that eats the heart of its very society. Many brothers and sisters in Zimbabwe have lost their souls for castles built upon pillars of sand. Many of them became wealthy by unscrupulous means, creating a society were there is only the aristocrats and everyone else.

Unfortunately, for my generation most of us are everyone else. If today, I found myself on my death bed I would die with anger and disappointment engraved in my heart. I would ask God why he allowed the wicked to prosper. I would ask Jesus WHY my generation never had an equal chance to pursue success and happiness in the land of our ancestors. Truly speaking we are a traumatized generation and I hope our leaders recognize and correct this ill before it degenerates into a time bomb. Zimbabwe is a land endowed with natural beauty and numerous resources yet Zimbabwe's children are scrounging in the trash bins of the economy to find food. Our reality of today is that we have been cheated of our destiny and we are very very angry and disappointed.

The *Patricians should give us an chance to set sail and design our own future in Zimbabwe. We deserve better. If you read Roman history you will know that the long struggle between the two orders(The *Patricians and the *Plebeians),ended in the attainment by the *Plebeians of political equality and the establishment of a new order made up of both classes. After this monumental achievement by the *Plebeians there were still problems facing the new order and I guess such is life. Conquering one massive challenge does not guarantee a life time in

*Neverland,challenges will continue emerging till the day we die and it is our part to deal with it. So,I have told you my life story.

There is no happy ending because I am still drifting on thin ice. Many of us are still struggling in the streets of Zimbabwe or crammed up in other peoples nations,working our butts off as economic immigrants,but in my heart I know that*Joshua is coming to take over from *Moses. The hour of divine appointment is drawing near and we must prepare to enter the promised land.

Indeed,every generation has it's own *prophet. I am yet to identify our generation's prophet and he lives in each and every one of us. When the time is right, you will see him and you will know him,but we must take heed because there will be many false prophets claiming to be our *Joshua. *Moses will hand over his stick of leadership to the new generation in the hour of divine appointment. *Moses has been to the mountaintop,he has seen the *promised land and It is beautiful. Unfortunately,he will not enter

the promised land because he sinned against God. Long live Zimbabwe!

THE FOLLOWING IS AN (UNEDITED) EXCERPT
FROM FRANKS NEXT BOOK, TITLED, LAND GRAB!

Land Grab!, looks at Zimbabwe's farm
invasions through the contrasting lives
of two man who were born on the same
Rhodesian farm in 1931. One the son of
a white farmer, the other, a poor native
laborer's son. They cross paths several
times in life, everything leading to one
final explosive moment, the land
grab. "Both man are aiming AK 47
Kalashnikov riffles at each other. John
refuses to leave and Shungu is adamant.
Both man are shouting, Get off my land!"

CHAPTER 1 EXCERPT:

(1931)It is a cold July evening on the vast Kenty Estate Farm,in Southern Rhodesia. Pete Townsend is pacing up and down on his mahogany tiled veranda of his 20 room farm house,scratching his crop of blond hair. He is anxiously smoking his pipe,a family heirloom that he inherited from his grandfather,the late General Sam Townsend.

On the other side of the farm,outside a cow dung plastered mud hut,Majoni is rolling a tobacco zoll with an old newspaper that he picked up from the boss's yard. He cant read,so the only use he has for a newspaper is to smoke tobacco in it. He is also anxious and waiting outside his mud hut,pacing up and down in his overalls and torn gumboots.

Minutes later,the cold July air is filled with the unmistakable cries of new life."Its a boy",exclaims the doctor to Peter Townsend. "Its a boy! Its a boy!",Pete Townsend's face beams with excitement as he promulgates the sweet glorious news.

"Chikomana!",the elderly compound midwife,Maduve,announces to Majoni,who is looking up to the heavens and thanking his ancestors for a healthy baby boy. "Lets celebrate,pour us some scotch boy!", Peter Townsend orders his butler, a frail seventy year old black native. "They are all boys, these bloody savages. You should always let them know who is the boss, whop them if you have to", his late father, Sam, used to tell him. John Townsend and Shungu Majoni are both born today, on the 4th of July on Kenty Estate Farm in the lush North Eastern province of Rhodesia.

Little John Townsend is wrapped in a brand new silk blanket and his father is holding him proudly in his arms. "All this land will be yours one day my son. All of it!", he whispers to his newborn son. "Ohhhh, look at those blue eyes, he has his grandfathers eyes", Pete's wife, Anne, says as she lies on the bed, recovering from the pains of childbirth. She is proud to have given Pete a heir to the vast Kenty Estate. "Lets call him John Townsend, he shall have the best education money can buy, to prepare him to take over this magnificent Estate", Pete says to his wife.

On the other side of the farm, Little Shungu Majoni is wrapped up in an old and torn out blanket that used to belong the boss's dog, Buck, who used to shit on it. "Ane zimhuno rababa vake chairo(he has a big nose like his father)"the elderly midwife,Maduve declares. Majoni holds his son in his arms,his face beaming with pride and joy,proclaiming,

"Ndishumba chaivo,Gurundoro homba huru,muzukuru wamambo Pfumoreropa(He is a true lion of the Gurundoro tribe,grandson of the great king Pfumoreropa)",in a loud voice. A small crowd gathers around his hut to offer their congratulations."Makorokoto edangwe Samusha (Congratulations on the first born)",they say to Majoni.

"Shungu!,anonzi Shungu!(Shungu!,his name is Shungu!",his mother,Chiwoniso, whispers in a faint voice. She has lost a lot of blood and her frail figure is exhausted from the labor pains. She closes her eyes to take a nap,but never to open them again. It is a very confusing day for Majoni today. He has just lost his beloved wife and he has also become a proud father."Inga murombo harovi chinenguwo (a poor man never gets a lucky break in this life)",the neighbors say to Majoni as they offer him their condolences for the sudden passing of his wife.

The next day,it's a hive of activity at the Townsend farm house. Family and friends from neighboring farms have come to celebrate the birth of the new Townsend. They are served tea and chocolate muffins in a spacious guest room, overlooking the green veld. Moments later, Pete emerges from the staircase into the spacious guest room, holding his little bundle of joy. "It's a boy!, his name is John Townsend, it's a healthy baby boy!", he proclaims to his equally amused guests.

"How wonderful Pete, this little lad will take over from you one day and continue the family legacy", Charles Meyer says. Charles Meyer is the wealthiest Rhodesian in these parts, with a fortune comprising of several farms, mining concessions and shares in the railroads. He was a friend of Cecil John Rhodes and helped pioneer the British South Africa Company. "We want you to be his godfather, Charlie", Peter says. "Oh that will be an honor", Charlie replies. They all drink a toast of the finest scotch whiskey to the bright future and good health of the new born.

Meanwhile, at the servants compound, there is a funeral. Majoni is burying his wife Chiwoniso, who passed away last night shortly after childbirth. Poor Shungu will never know his mother. The midwife who helped deliver him into the world,Maduve,is clutching him in her arms and sobbing uncontrollably for her deceased friend. Chiwoniso's final resting place is a shallow,unmarked grave. It was dug in a jiffy as the natives had to go back to work in the Kenty Estate tobacco fields.

There is no time to spend the day attending funerals,if Pete Townsend finds out,they will be hell to pay. Everyone has a quota of tobacco they must pick everyday. Those who fail to fulfill their quota are usually tied to a tree and fledged mercilessly in full view of the whole native compound.

Maduve,the midwife,is the only person who was allowed to retire from working in the fields. She is now responsible for performing household chores at Pete Townsend's farm house. "Don't worry Majoni,i will look after your child like he is my own,i will feed him goat milk,go on and fulfill your tobacco quota before you get in trouble",Chiwoniso says to a grief stricken and inconsolable Majoni who is still trying to comprehend the full measure of his sudden loss. "Rimwe zuva,zvichavawanawo mabhunuaya,rimwezuva ka!(ONE day these whites will pay,one day!),Majoni replies.

Everyone in the compound knows who

Majoni is,but it's a well kept secret in order to protect him from the Townsend's fury. Majoni is the only surviving son of King Gurundoro Pfumoreropa,who once ruled these lands before the invasion by white settlers. Majoni wobbles in agony to the tobacco fields to fulfill his quota. The boss,Pete Townsend wouldn't care less for a dead Nigga's wife."They are animals,they must work",he always says.

Such is the world Shungu Majoni and John Townsend are born in. It is a racially segregated world,where the white man fancies himself God over the native blacks. Kenty Estate Farm is a pride and joy of the Townsend's and a nightmare for the Majoni's. Toddlers, Johny and Shungu do not know about this arrangement in the outside world. They are both innocent like any new born. However,it is in growing up they will discover their differences. It will be a particularly hard lesson for Shungu and an embarrassing one for John Townsend.

Maduve who has taken the role of mother to Shungu,often takes him along to the Townsend's farm house. One day,another little toddler,Johny,crawls towards Shungu and they start playing together,in typical toddler fashion.

Pete Townsend notices this and orders Maduve not to bring that "animal child" into his house again. "That bastard of a dog child will bring my son diseases,keep him away from here",he says

The next day,Maduve comes to do her household chores,leaving Shungu behind at the native compound. Weirdly enough,little John Townsend starts crying for the company of his new found friend. He wont stop crying and finally his mother gives in to the heirs demands. "Pete,let Maduve bring that native boy so that John can play with him,he wont stop crying. He longs for company of his own age",she pleads with Pete who reluctantly agrees. "But,make sure that boy is washed before he is brought to this house!",he barks to Maduve. "O-Right,Sir and Madam",Maduve replies in the only english she can muster.

The next couple of years,Maduve brings little Shungu to play with the bosses son. It is at the Madams house that Shungu learns to speak fluent english. One day,six year old Shungu and Johny are playing *horse and rider,*one of their favorite games on the front porch. This day however,Shungu is the horse and Johny the rider. Majoni and

Pete Townsend both happen to notice this. Majoni is trimming the bosses exotic hedge and Pete is sitting on his rocking chair, smoking a cigar, on the veranda of his farm house. "Go on my boy, ride that Nigga!, they are stubborn mules his kind, hit him!", Pete Townsend proudly cheers to his son. For Majoni, watching this event is demeaning and devastating.

Majoni decides it's time to have a little chat with his son. Pete Townsend's is also thinking the same thing. Majoni completes his back breaking task and leaves for the native compound. A little later, Maduve arrives at the compound with a tired Shungu sleeping on her back. "Wake him up", Majoni orders Maduve. "I need to talk to my son." Shungu wakes up and sits on a wooden stool. His father is steering a rusty pot of pap (milie meal) on a small fire in the center of their mud hut. Todays pap will be served with salt. Majoni cant afford to buy meat or vegetables. The wild worms they sometimes eat with the pap are finished. They will have to wait until next spring, when the worms start breeding in the harati tree.

"My son, there are some things you need to know about your friend Johny and his

family. Son, we are not the same with the Townsend's. They are cracker heads and they treat us with utter disrespect. A long time ago, your grandfather, my father, Mambo Pfumoreropa was the king of these lands. He ruled his people justly and fairly. The people had their own fields and cattle and they had a sustainable lifestyle. Things were different back then. Our family is a royal family of the Gurundoro people. Our ancestors lived in these lands long before the white man came. Your grandfather was the first son of his father, Muvhimi Gurundoro. Back then, young people had to be initiated into manhood and it was formidably tougher for young royals.

One day, the village elders took a group of young men for an initiation ceremony up in the Makumimavi mountains. They stayed there for several days learning the sacred ways of the Gurundoro people. Our people were proud hunters and each boy had to prove this. The last initiation task into manhood was a hunting expedition. Each boy was given one day to go and hunt for a strong animal to prove his worth to the tribe. Your grandfather, Pfumoreropa ventured deep into the forest and he encountered a hungry white lion. The white lion is

a very rare and fierce animal.
The other boys fled the scene but your grandfather stood like a man with a spear in his right hand. When the lion leaps towards him, he trust his spear into its heart with such brute force, the lion died instantly. He carried the dead lion on his shoulders and herded to the royal compound where the elders and villagers were waiting. The whole village watched in awe as Pfumoreropa carried a white lion on his shoulders. His father, Muvhimi Gurundoro, came out to meet him at the royal compound entrance. His mother, Hazvinei was ululating for her brave warrior son along with the other village ladies. Your grandfather, Pfumoreropa proved himself worthy to rule the Gurundoro people that day. He gained the respect of his father and everyone else in the kingdom.
The elders skinned the lion and made a royal garment with the lions skin for Pfumoreropa. In a secret ceremony, that night, Pfumoreropa ate the raw heart of the lion in front of the elders. This was meant to give him strength over his enemies. That night the people celebrated for the glorious young royal. There was plenty of beer and food. The people ate until their

stomachs could eat no more.

Years later,King Muvhimi died of old age and Pfumoreropa ascended to the throne. He married the most beautiful bride in the kingdom,Queen Kumbirai of the Soko people. His wedding was yet another glorious day that the kingdom celebrated their new king.

Pfumoreropa ruled justly and fairly and the people loved him. One day,in the year of 1988,four white man came to our lands riding on horse backs. Our people thought they had come to trade but these man had a paper which they gave to King Pfumoreropa. They said that the paper was from the Great King Lobengula who owned all the lands of these parts. They said that this Lobengula King had given them authority to take over the Gurundoro lands.

Pfumoreropa refused to acknowledge this rubbish news and the white man were infuriated. The Gurundoro people only had one King and it was Pfumoreropa. They had never heard of a King Lobengula. The white man left and threatened to come back with an army. Pfumoreropa accepted the challenge. He had the best spear throwing soldiers in the land. His man were fit and strong and they were prepared to fight to death for their land. Mambo

Pfumoreropa's land was fertile and he was not about to give it to anyone without a fight. The land belonged to his people. His ancestors had lived and prospered in these lands. In the next few weeks a war broke out between the white man and the Gurundoro people. The white mans army was led by a General Sam Townsend, an evil man who had no respect for native life.

Unfortunately the white devils had a superior weapon. They had the stick that spits fire(guns). They shot and killed many man of the Gurundoro kingdom. Pfumoreropa went in hiding with a small band of man, up in the Makumimavi mountains. General Sam Townsend bombed the mountain with dynamite and King Pfumoreropa surrendered. He was captured alive and they bound him with ropes and chains and dragged him to the village.

They tied him to a big mahogany tree and left him there for three days. None was allowed to give him any water or food. The people watched in agony and disgrace as their king suffered for three days. His wife, Kumbirai tried to bring him water and she was shot in the head by General Townsend's man. She died right there on the spot a few feet from where your grandfather, Pfumoreropa was tied. On the third day,General Sam Townsend gathered the whole village around the mahogany tree where Pfumoreropa was tied. He tied a rope around Pfumoreropa's neck and hanged him. I was just a young boy back then and the people had hid me with the Soko people who lived beyond the mountains.

My father,your grandfather,died at the hands of your good friend,John Townsend's grandfather,the evil General Sam Townsend. Our peoples land was taken away and divided into large farms for these white man. This farm land of Kenty Estate is just a small part of what used to be our peoples Kingdom. A year after Pfumoreropa's death General Sam Townsend and his man conquered the Soko people as well. Everyone, including myself,was forced to work on the land for the whites. The white devils divided the kingdoms into vast farms.

Unfortunately for me,I was part of the group that was forced to work on General Townsend's farm. Thankfully,the Soko people have kept my identity hidden for all these years. That is our history son. That is how we came to be here. We were captured and forced to work against our will. The white man took our land,our cattle and our dignity. *Never ever trust a white man, you hear. Do not for one second think that John is your friend. You heard what his father Pete was saying today. Remember my son, never ever trust a white man. I don't want to see you playing with that spoiled brat again. You are now old enough to come and work with us in the fields but I will ask Pete Townsend if he can allow you to go and study at the Roman Catholic mission. I want you to learn the white man's knowledge and use it against them one day. Your task is to restore the pride of the Gurundoro people one day. Remember that!"*

On the other side of the farm, Pete Townsend is having dinner with his family on a Victorian dining table. The butler has prepared Johns favorite, Mutton sauce served on a bed of fresh rice. Pete is essentially proud of his son today for riding that native boy like a horse. *"Son, there are things you need to know about us Townsend's. We are a superior family and our race is superior to these native dogs. Your grandfather came to this country in 1888 from Britain, with nothing but a dream. He became a decorated army general and he led a battalion of courageous man to kill*

these black savages and restore order
in Africa. He fought many of these
black savages and killed them all. This
land which is now our farm was a savage
kingdom of some stubborn Gurundoro
King. That savage king cost your
grandfather the lives of several man in
his battalion.

However, your grandfather, Sam Townsend
hunted down that savage King and they
captured him in the Mountains. To
install law and order, he tied that
savage king to a tree and hanged him in
front of all the blacks. After that
there were few resistances from other
savage Kings as they feared the fate of
that Gurundoro. Your grandfather
restored peace and order in these
lands, allowing multitudes of white
settlers to come to this country. Sam
Townsend was a hero, a bold man who
served his white community with
dignity.

The white race is the only superior
race on this planet. These darkies are
nothing but savages. They are monkeys
and all they are good for is work.
Thats why we don't pay them anything.
If you don't keep them working they
will only steal from you or kill you if
they get the chance. They are domicile
low lives. They are not human. From

today on,i don't want to see you playing with that savage boy. Since he is your childhood pet friend I will allow him to go to the Missionary school to be taught to become a cook. I am proud of you for riding that Nigga. Now eat up your Mutton soup before it gets cold"

Early in the morning,a white man comes galloping on his high horse to the native compound. The only time the whites come to the compound is when someone is getting a beating. The natives are tense and there is an eerie silence."Shungu Majoni,where the hell can I find a boy by that name?", announces the white rider. Maduve comes out clutching the boy in her arms. "Please don't kill him Sir,He is good boy,he working hard one day,you will see",Maduve pleads with the strange white rider. "Shut up savage!,you only speak when you are spoken to. I want that boy. He is coming with me to the Mission School to study for a cook. Bring him here",the white rider orders.

At a private school at Charlie Meyers farm a young boy is being introduced to the class. He is wearing a nice fitting blue and Grey uniform and his crop of blond hair is well comped. He is nervous,but excited at the same time."Class,let us welcome John Townsend. He will be joining our class from today. Please John,have a seat",an elderly Mrs Van Wyk announces. She is a school teacher for this private,whites only school that was established by Charlie Meyer."Todays lesson is Classical piano. Who would like to play something for us",Mrs Van Wyk announces to her class.

Under a *Muchakata* tree,a small class of native boys is sitting on dusty gravel sand. The chalk board is fixed to the base of the tree with barbed wire. The missionary priest,Father Walter walks towards the tree with a frail and timid looking native boy. "Class,this is our new friend Shungu,please make him feel at home. He shall be studying with us for the following years",father Walter announces to a class of amused native kids. Shungu sits down next to Tawanda Mabhandi,a boy who will later become his best friend."Our lesson today is the english alphabet. If you are going to become a cook you will need to speak good english",the Missionary teacher announces. Having no pen or paper,the native kids start writing the alphabet on the gravel sand.

Over the next thirteen years Shungu and John complete their primary and secondary school. They have never met again since that day when they last played horse and rider. They are now both nineteen years old and fully aware of the differences between blacks and whites. Shungu always talks about his white friend that he grew up playing with,but John Townsend never mentions that he once played with a Nigga,as a child. It's an embarrassment to him. Both,Shungu and John have passed their secondary level with flying colors.

Father Walter thinks that making Shungu an ordinary cook will be wasting the boys talents. "This young native has great potential. He is very intelligent",he says to the other missionaries. Father Walter decides that Shungu should be send to England to study medicine and become a doctor for the natives.

Pete Townsend is happy his son has completed secondary school today."Son,i guess you know that all this land will be yours one day. I want you to become my apprentice and learn all about the farming business. I have a present for you outside,it's a the latest Henry Ford pick up truck. John is so astonished by the automobile. Only Charlie Meyer has one in this parts. He is determined to learn the farming business. He wants to prove to his father that he is a true Townsend.

Over the next ten years Shungu studies medicine at Oxford University in England and Johny becomes a master at the farming business. In London,Shungu befriends some white folks and learns the way of the white man. His father cannot write or read so he writes letters to Father Walter,who in turn reads them to Shungu's father. On the day of his graduation,he receives a letter from Father Walter.

"Dear Shungu. I am writing this letter under instruction from your father. He told me to tell you.....*Son, I hope our ancestors are keeping you safe in that land of the white man. Back here,nothing much has changed. The new boss,John Townsend is even more ruthless than his father. Last week he beat up Maduve. She died the next day in her hut. We hope you will return soon and cure our people. Father Walter told me that you are studying the white mans medicine. I pray that you return safely my son. Remember,you are the grandson of Mambo Pfumoreropa. Your people need you. I love you my son. Your father. Majoni.*"

ABOUT THE AUTHOR

Tendai Frank Tagarira is a young Zimbabwean writer. He is 25 years old and plans to get in the World Book of Records as the most prolific young African writer. Currently he has writen the following published titles:

1. Beyond Money,Parable of the Pumpkin Seeds (Self Help/Inspirational)

2. Trying To Make Sense of It (Autobiography)

3. Savoring the Moment and Monologue of Consciousness (Creative Literature)

4.Land Grab (Novel)

5. African Beer hall Stories (Short Stories)

All the titles were writen in 2008/2009. Tendai is planning several other titles. His dream is to write at least 30 books by the time he is 30 years. He is currently 25 years of age.